£1.00

£1.00

Why Why Why can't penguins fly?

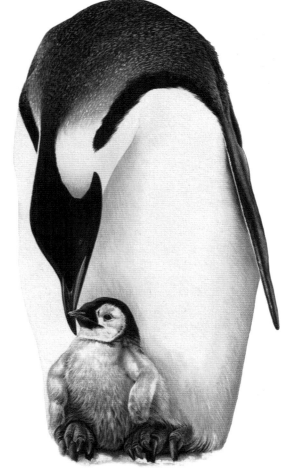

Miles Kelly

PUBLISHING

First published in 2005 by
Miles Kelly Publishing Ltd
Bardfield Centre, Great Bardfield, Essex, CM7 4SL

Copyright © Miles Kelly Publishing Ltd 2005

2 4 6 8 10 9 7 5 3 1

Editorial Director
Belinda Gallagher

Art Director
Jo Brewer

Editorial Assistant
Amanda Askew

Author
Camilla de la Bedoyere

Volume Designer
Jo Brewer

Indexer
Helen Snaith

Production Manager
Estela Boulton

Scanning and Reprographics
Anthony Cambray, Mike Coupe, Ian Paulyn

ISBN 1-84236-603-3

Printed in China

British Library Cataloguing-in-Publication Data
A catalogue record for this book is available
from the British Library

www.mileskelly.net
info@mileskelly.net

Contents

What is special about birds?

Birds can fly, walk, run and even swim! Because they have wings, birds are able to fly to all parts of the world, from steamy rainforests to the icy Arctic. There are about 9000 different types of bird, from beautiful barn owls to giant ostriches.

Do birds have teeth?

Birds don't have teeth. Instead, they have really strong mouths that are called beaks, or bills. Sharp, pointed beaks are good for grabbing bugs and short, strong beaks are great for cracking nuts open!

Discover

Beaks and feathers are made of a special tough material. See if you can you discover what it's called.

Barn owl

Why do birds lay eggs?

Birds lay eggs so that their babies can grow. Baby birds are called chicks and they begin life in an egg. The eggs are kept safe in a nest until they hatch.

Song thrush

Eggs in a nest

5

Which is the biggest bird?

The ostrich is the world's biggest bird. The tallest ostriches reach nearly 3 metres in height and can weigh twice as much as an adult human! Although ostriches have wings and their bodies are covered in fluffy feathers, they are far too heavy to fly.

Big bird!

The great bustard is the world's largest flying bird. It measures up to one metre in length and can weigh as much as 20 kilograms. That's the same weight as a five-year-old child!

Ostrich

What bird has the biggest wings?

Birds can spread their wings and glide on the wind like a kite. Albatrosses are very good flyers because they have the largest wingspan (the measurement from wing-tip to wing-tip) of any bird. Their wingspan may measure up to 3.3 metres.

Albatross

Measure
Using a measuring tape, find out how tall an ostrich is. Its height is on page 6.

Why is a hummingbird so tiny?

Hummingbirds are tiny so that they can reach inside flowers. They feed on the sweet juice, called nectar, which flowers make. The bee hummingbird is the world's smallest bird. It measures only 5 centimetres and weighs less than a spoonful of rice!

How do birds fly?

Birds can fly because they have wings, powerful muscles and very light bones. Feathers also help birds move smoothly through the air. This peregrine falcon is the fastest of all animals. It can reach top speeds of 180 kilometres an hour as it swoops and dives.

Peregrine falcon

How far can a bird fly?

Birds can fly very long distances. Swifts are super fliers and even eat and mate while they swoop through the clouds. When young swifts leave the nest they may fly for the next two years and travel more than 500,000 kilometres!

Count
If a bird beats its wings ten times in one second, how many times would it beat its wings in two seconds?

Do all birds fly?

All birds have wings, but not all of them fly. This speedy roadrunner lives in the desert. It can fly, but it prefers to walk or run as it looks for lizards, snakes and bugs in the sand.

Roadrunner

Swift

Hum that tune!

Hummingbirds beat their wings 50 times a second. As the wings slice through the air they make the humming noise that gives the birds their name.

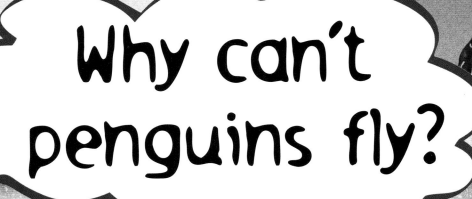

Why can't penguins fly?

Penguins can't fly because their wings are too short and stumpy. They use their tiny wings like flippers to help them dive into icy water at the Antarctic. Penguins don't need to fly because they are great swimmers and can find plenty of food underwater.

Emperor penguin

Gentoo penguin

Can penguins swim fast?

Some penguins can swim fast. The gentoo penguin can swim up to 27 kilometres an hour – faster than most people can run! Penguins swim well because they have smooth bodies, webbed feet and flipper-like wings.

How do seabirds catch fish?

Seabirds live near the ocean, which is packed full of fish and other treats. Gannets need good eyesight to spot fish just below the water's surface. When they have seen something interesting, they dive into the water and grab it in their beaks.

Super sliders!

Penguins may be great swimmers, but they are clumsy walkers. When waddling takes too long, they jump on to their bellies and slide along the ice instead!

Northern gannet

Explore

Penguins live at the freezing Antarctic. Look at an atlas to find out where the Antarctic is.

King penguin

Why are some birds colourful?

Birds can be big show-offs and they use bright colours to make themselves look attractive. Male birds are usually more colourful than females.

When this peacock sees a female (a peahen) he displays his fine tail and shakes it, so she can admire his great beauty.

Love birds!

Great crested grebes are water birds that dance for each other. During the dance they offer each other gifts – beakfuls of water weed. Lovely!

Peacock

Which birds strut around and coo?

Male birds puff up their feathers, strut around and make cooing noises to impress the females. These cocks-of-the-rocks also dance and spread their wings to show off to the female birds. They live in the South American rainforest.

Cocks-of-the-rocks

Why do birds sing?

Birds sing to get the attention of other birds. Like their colourful feathers, they may use songs to attract mates. Some birds squawk loudly if they are being attacked. Most baby birds learn to sing by copying their parents.

Dress-up

A bird's feathers are called its plumage. Put on some bright clothes and see if anyone notices your plumage!

Why do birds lay eggs in nests?

Birds lay their eggs in a nest to keep them safe. Once the eggs have hatched, the little chicks stay in the nest until they have grown enough to be able to fly. These bald eagles build giant nests up to 2.5 metres across.

Bald eagle

Chicks

Why are cuckoos lazy?

Cuckoos don't bother making their own nests. Instead, they lay their eggs in other birds' nests. This way cuckoos do not have all the hard work of looking after their own chicks — other birds do it for them!

How do birds build nests?

Birds build their nests in different ways, but most of them use twigs and sticks. African weaver birds make their delicate nests using strips of leaves and grass. They knot and weave the strips together to make a cosy, safe home.

Make it

Use sticks and twigs to make a nest. Make a soft lining with grass or straw. Pop some chocolate eggs in the middle.

1. The weaver bird twists strips of leaves

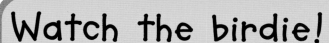

2. The roof is made

Watch the birdie!

Most birds take minutes to lay an egg. The mother cuckoo can lay an egg in 9 seconds! This allows her to quickly pop it in the nest of another bird.

3. The finished nest

When is a bird like a sponge?

A bird is like a sponge when it can soak up water!
Sandgrouses live in dry deserts and when they find a pool of water they lie in it. The feathers on their tummies soak up the water, which the birds can then take back to their thirsty chicks.

Vultures

Sand grouse

Why do vultures look so peculiar?

Vultures do not have feathers on their heads and necks. They feed on dead animals and their heads are feather-free so they don't get messy when they eat! Vultures have good eyesight so they can spot dead animals from far away.

Which bird lives in a cactus?

The tiny elf owl from America sometimes makes its home in a prickly cactus. This might be uncomfortable for the bird, but it does help keep its eggs and chicks safe from any lizards or snakes that might want to eat them.

Bone-crusher bird!

Vultures are birds that eat mainly dead animals. The lammergeier vulture even munches on bones. It drops big bones onto rocks to smash them into pieces before eating them.

Find out

Find out the name for special places in the desert where there is water and plants can grow.

What is a bird of prey?

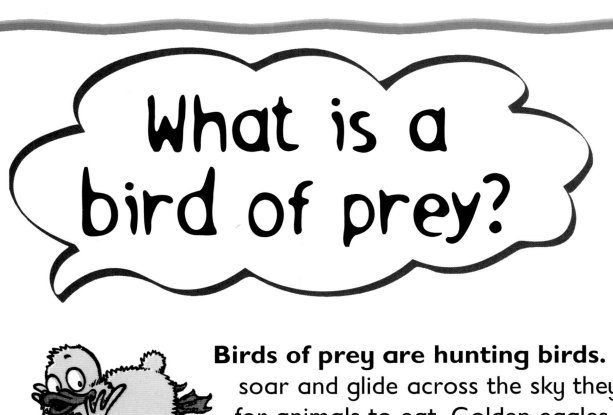

Birds of prey are hunting birds. As they soar and glide across the sky they search for animals to eat. Golden eagles have extremely good eyesight and can spot food far away. They swoop to the ground and grab rabbits and mice with their sharp claws.

Golden eagle

Top bird!

Eagles like to build their nests in high places. One pair of sea eagles made their nest on top of a light–tower by the coast in Norway!

How does a sea eagle catch fish?

Sea eagles need good eyes and strong claws to catch a swimming fish. Each foot has a pointed hook for holding onto a slippery fish. Sea eagles take their fish to a cliff or rocky ledge where they can eat in comfort.

Sea eagle

Do hunting birds live in towns?

It's unusual to see big hunting birds such as eagles in towns. But you might see smaller ones, such as ravens. These black birds are very clever animals. They hunt mice and rats but they will eat almost any food that they can find.

Try it

Eagles use their feet to grab their food. See if you can pick up anything using just your feet.

How do birds look after their chicks?

Chicks are an easy target for other animals that may want to eat them. Their parents have to take special care of them. When ducklings hatch from their eggs they stay close to their parents and follow them everywhere.

Mallard duck

Why do birds sit on their eggs?

Birds sit on their eggs to keep them warm. Eggs need to be warm for the chicks to grow. Emperor penguins keep their eggs cosy by holding them off the ice. They rest the eggs on their feet, beneath a flap of skin and feathers.

Chilled-out birds!

Penguins huddle together to warm themselves and their eggs. They even take it in turns to stand on the edge of the group and brave the cold winds!

1. Egg starts to crack

2. Chick breaks out

3. Egg splits open

4. Chick wriggles free

Discover

Eggs are an unusual shape to stop them rolling away. Place an egg on a table and see how far it rolls.

How does a chick grow inside an egg?

Inside an egg, the white, clear liquid protects a chick from bumps and knocks. Yellow yolk contains goodness to help the chick grow. The hard shell keeps the chick safe. When it is ready to hatch, the chick breaks its way out of the egg.

Is it true that parrots can talk?

Parrots are intelligent birds that can copy all sorts of sounds – including us! Scarlet macaws live in the hot and steamy rainforests of South America. They live in large groups (called flocks) and they screech and squawk loudly to one another.

Quetzal

Scarlet macaw

What is the most beautiful bird?

The quetzal is one of the most beautiful birds. The male has shiny green feathers and a bright red chest. His tail feathers sail behind him as he flies.

Jungle fowl

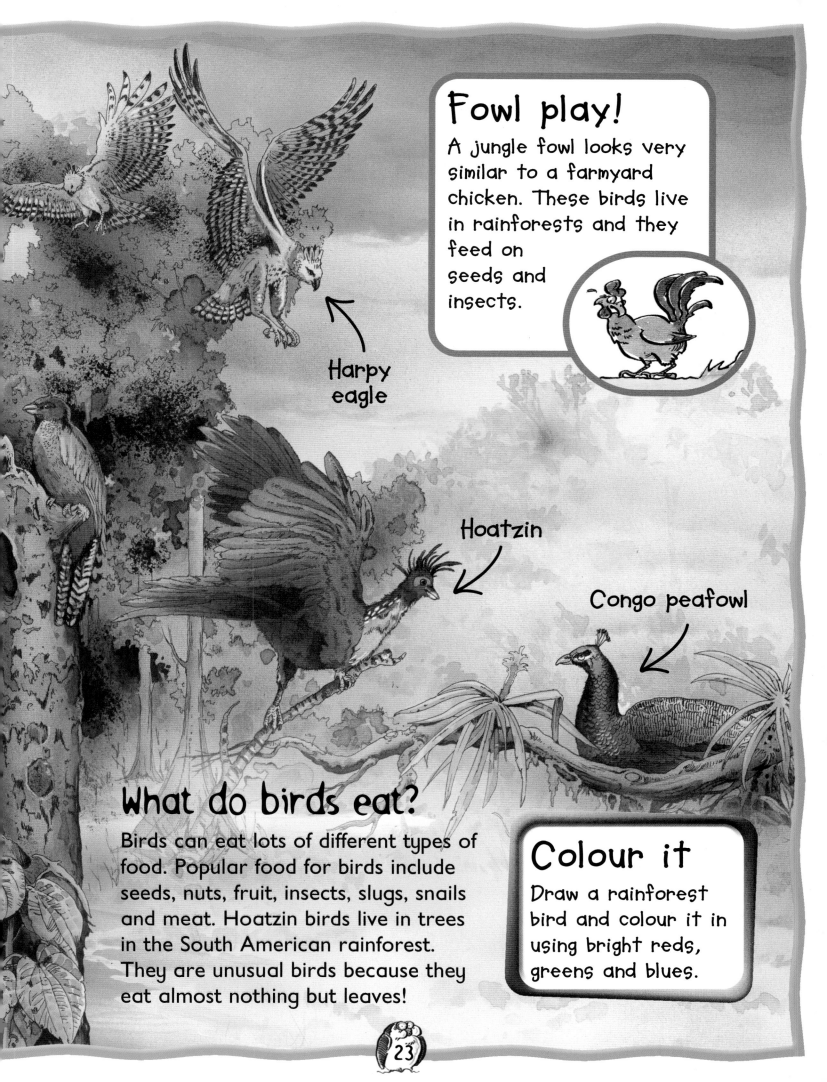

Fowl play!

A jungle fowl looks very similar to a farmyard chicken. These birds live in rainforests and they feed on seeds and insects.

Harpy eagle

Hoatzin

Congo peafowl

What do birds eat?

Birds can eat lots of different types of food. Popular food for birds include seeds, nuts, fruit, insects, slugs, snails and meat. Hoatzin birds live in trees in the South American rainforest. They are unusual birds because they eat almost nothing but leaves!

Colour it

Draw a rainforest bird and colour it in using bright reds, greens and blues.

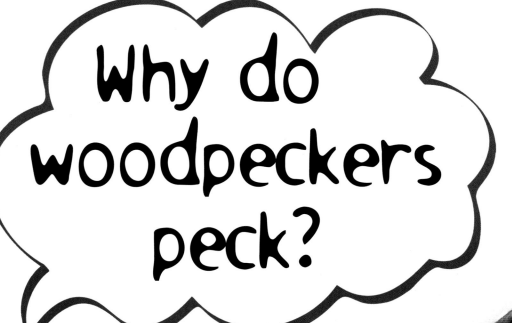

Why do woodpeckers peck?

Woodpeckers peck at trees to disturb the little insects that live in the bark. They then gobble them up. These birds can also use their strong, pointed beaks to hammer at the tree until they have made a hole big enough for a nest.

Hummm, I'm hungry!

Bee hummingbirds beat their wings 200 times a second. If we used up the same amount of energy we would need to eat three times our own weight in potatoes each day!

How do honeyguides find their food?

Honeyguide birds follow honey badgers to find their favourite food – delicious bee grubs! The clever birds follow the badgers when they go in search of a bee's nest. When the badger opens the nest it feeds on the honey, while the birds eat the grubs and beeswax.

Honeyguide

Make it

Ask an adult to help you make a bird feeder. You can then hang it upside down from a tree.

Do antbirds eat ants?

Antbirds follow army ants as they march through the forest, but they don't usually eat them. The birds perch on trees as the army ants pass by, then they pounce on the other small animals and insects that come to feed on the ants.

Why is a snowy owl coloured white?

Snowy owls live near the freezing Arctic where there is snow and ice. Because their feathers are mostly white they can perch on the ground and stay hidden. This means they can hunt animals such as hares without being seen.

Snowy owl

Why do some birds travel to warmer lands?

Many birds travel away from cold areas during winter. Tundra swans live near the cold Arctic in summer, but when the weather gets worse they fly to warmer places to find food.

Do penguins get wet and cold?

Penguins live at the freezing South Pole. They have special feathers that are coated in oil to keep water off their bodies. They also have a thick layer of fat under their skin. When they are on land, penguins huddle together to keep warm.

High flier!

The Canada goose spends summer in the Arctic and flies south in winter. This way the bird gets warm weather all year round!

Emperor penguin

Tundra swan

Think

Animals in snowy areas are often white. What colours would be best for animals living in forests?

How does a bird eat a snail?

Birds that eat snails need to get the soft body out of the hard shell. Some birds smash snails against rocks. This snail kite uses its sharp beak to cut the slimy snail away from its shell and hook it out.

Knobbly knees!

Flamingos look as if they have got back-to-front legs. Actually, what appear to be their knees are really their ankles!

Snail kite

Which bird has a scissor-shaped beak?

The beak of a skimmer is shaped like scissors. This is because the lower beak is much longer and flatter than the top beak. As it flies over water, the skimmer dips its lower beak below the surface. When it touches a fish it snaps its beak shut.

Flamingo

Why do flamingos have long necks?

Flamingos have long necks so that they can reach underwater to find their food. They use their beaks to catch tiny pink creatures called shrimps that float past. Flamingos turn pink after eating lots of these shrimps!

Remember

Can you remember what a skimmer's beak is shaped like? If you can't, read this page again to find out.

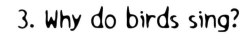

Quiz time

Do you remember what you have read about birds? These questions will test your memory. The pictures will help you. If you get stuck, read the pages again.

page 5

1. Why do birds lay eggs?

3. Why do birds sing?

page 13

4. How do birds build nests?

page 15

5. Why are cuckoos lazy?

page 15

2. How far can a bird fly?

page 8

6. When is a bird like a sponge?

page 16

7. What is a bird of prey?

page 18

8. Do antbirds eat ants?

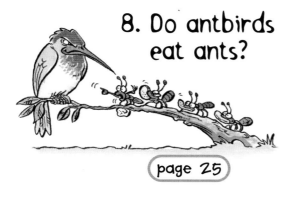

page 25

9. Which bird lives in a cactus?

page 17

10. How does a chick grow inside an egg?

page 21

11. Why do woodpeckers peck?

page 24

page 19

12. Do hunting birds live in towns?

page 29

13. Why do flamingos have long necks?

Answers

1. So their babies can grow
2. Very long distances
3. To get the attention of other birds
4. With twigs and sticks
5. Because they don't make their own nests
6. When the sandgrouse soaks up water with its feathers
7. A hunting bird
8. Yes, they eat army ants
9. The elf owl
10. The yolk contains goodness to help the chick grow
11. To disturb insects in the tree so they can eat them
12. Yes, smaller ones do
13. So they can reach underwater to find their food

Index